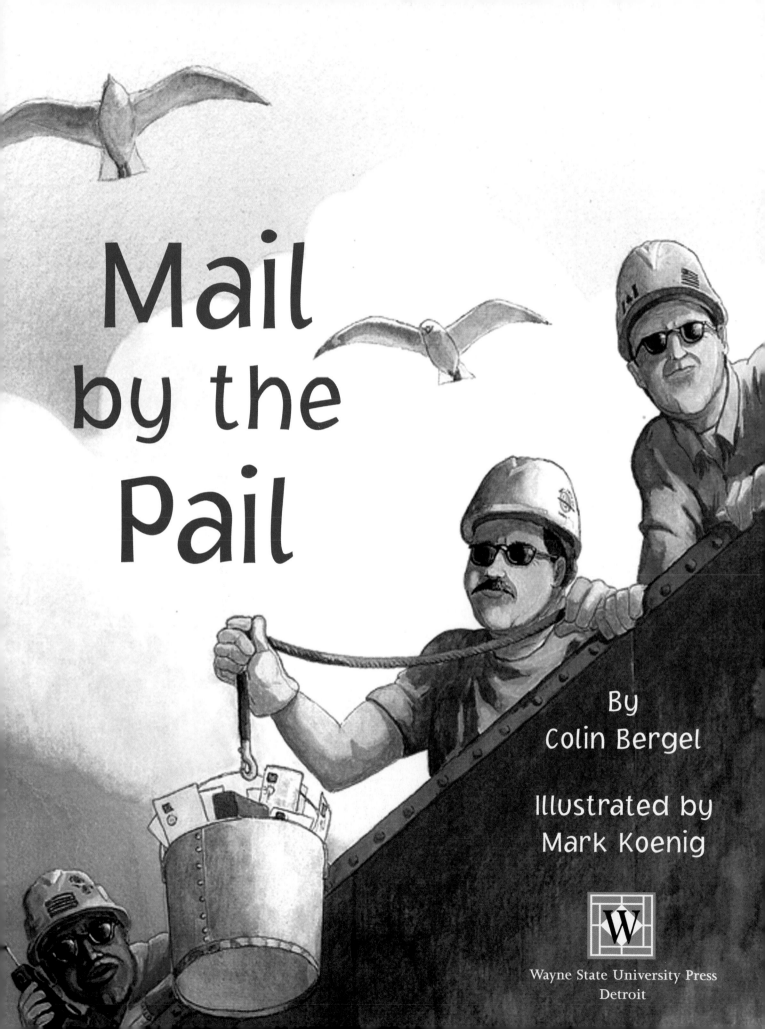

Mail by the Pail

By
Colin Bergel

Illustrated by
Mark Koenig

Wayne State University Press
Detroit

Great Lakes Books

Dr. Charles K. Hyde
Department of History, Wayne State University

A complete listing of the books in this series can be found online at wsupress.wayne.edu

18 17 16 15 14   7 6 5 4 3

ISBN-13: 978-0-8143-2890-3

Pages designed and typeset by Calabria Design

Library of Congress Cataloging-in-Publication Data

Bergel, Colin 1963-
   Mail by the pail / by Colin Bergel ; illustrated by Mark Koenig.
      p. cm.
Summary: A young girl learns how the birthday card she makes for her father will get to him as he works on a freighter carrying coal on Lake Michigan.
   ISBN 0-8143-2890-3 -- ISBN 0-8143-2891-1 (pbk.)
   [1. Postal service--Michigan, Lake--Fiction. 2. Ship letters--Fiction.
3. Fathers and daughters--Fiction.] I. Koenig, Mark, ill. II. Title.
   PZ7.B44975 Mai 2000
   [E]--dc21
                              00-009687

To my wife, Joyce,
and our children,
Ian, Kayla, and Emily

On the eastern shore of Lake Michigan is the
small port city of Manistee, Michigan.

In Manistee, in an old Victorian house at 332 West 45th Street, lives a little girl who wonders about each ship that comes into port. Her name is Mary.

Mary's dad is a sailor who works on a big ship called a *lake freighter*. Lake freighters are huge—as long as two or three football fields—but most people on the Great Lakes call even the largest freighter a boat. The name of her dad's boat is the *Big Laker*. The *Big Laker* carries cargo like iron ore, stone, and coal to many ports on the Great Lakes.

When Mary's dad is working, he is away from home for many weeks at a time. Hanging on a wall in his room on the *Big Laker* is a calendar. On the calendar he keeps track of the number of days he has worked and how many days are left before he can go home to see Mary and her mom.

Every so often, when the *Big Laker* delivers coal to Manistee, Mary gets to see her dad while the coal is being unloaded. That always makes her happy. She and her mom go down to the dock to meet him. Then they take a stroll along the river, enjoying ice cream or a box of chocolate fudge. But it takes only a few hours to unload the *Big Laker*. Usually, by the time they are finished with their snacks, it's time for Mary's dad to go back to the boat.

Mary misses her dad when he is away working. She misses him a lot. One day, when he had been away on the *Big Laker* for five weeks, Mary was feeling especially sad. Her mom walked into the room with a letter in her hand. It was for Mary, and it was from her dad!

Lake Huron
September 7

Dear Mary,

How's my little girl? Is school going well for you? As you know, my cell phone is still broken, and we've been getting into the docks in the middle of the night or during work, so I haven't had a chance to call home for a few days. Two days ago it rained while we were unloading stone in Superior, Wisconsin, and even with my rain gear on I was completely soaked! Then we moved over that night and loaded iron ore at the chute dock in Duluth, Minnesota. It was sunny but a little cool when we went through the Soo Locks this morning. Tomorrow we will get into Cleveland, Ohio, late at night again, so I figured I would not get a chance to talk to you until next week, when I get back to a dock up on Lake Superior.

Now I have good news and bad news. First, the bad news. My vacation is going to be delayed about two weeks, so I won't be home for my birthday. I have to wait until one of the other sailors gets back before I can come home. The good news is that the Captain said we might be going to pick up a load of coal for Manistee. We'll have to wait and see. Anyway, I miss you very much and can't wait to see you! Be good for your mom, and take care.

Love,
Dad

Mary's mom saw her daughter's face fall. "What's wrong?" she asked.

"Dad's going to miss his birthday with us," Mary replied, frowning. Then she got a great idea. "I'm going to send Daddy a birthday card." She paused. "But how will the card get to him? We don't even know where he is, so where do we send it?"

Mary's mom pointed to the envelope in her hand and said, "Do you notice anything unusual next to the stamp?" Mary looked closely at the envelope. Between the stamp and her dad's name was a picture of a little boat. Printed carefully under the little boat was the word "Mailboat." Then her mother asked, "Did you know that your daddy gets his mail by a pail?"

Mary looked puzzled. Mail by the pail? What did that mean?
She began to imagine all sorts of strange things.

Her mom explained. "Sending a card to a sailor on a boat was not always as easy as it is today. In the early days of shipping on the Great Lakes, boats received mail or messages only when they were at a dock. Then, in 1874, Mr. John W. Westcott started a delivery business.

He used a small rowboat to deliver messages to boats moving slowly on the Detroit River. Mr. Westcott's business grew quickly, and before long, Mr. Westcott was delivering mail and packages, too."

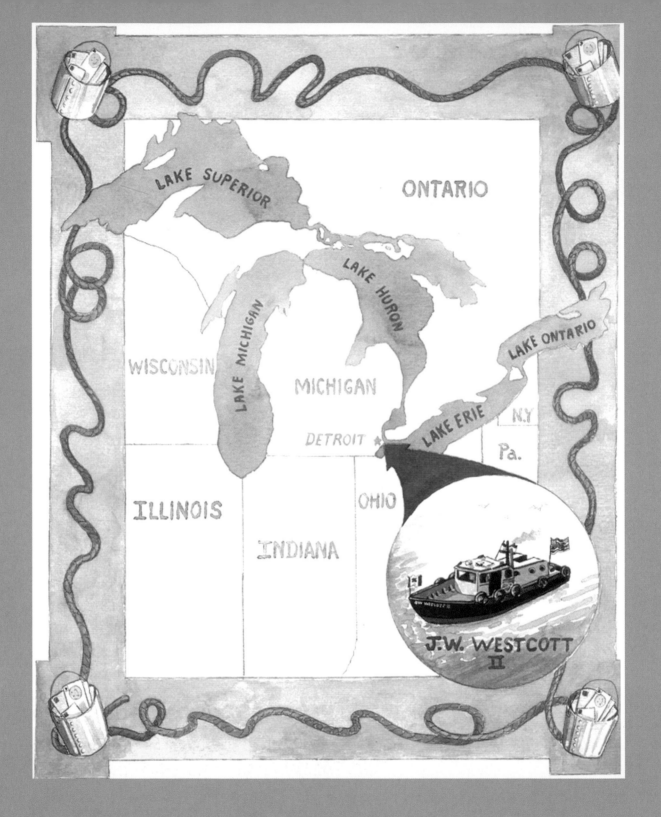

"So if I send a letter to Mr. Westcott, he'll know how to find dad's boat?" Mary asked.

Her mom chuckled. "Not exactly. Today, the mail for the *Big Laker*, as well as for many other boats on the Great Lakes, is sent to the marine post office in Detroit, Michigan. It is then sorted and held there until each boat passes by."

"So how does the mail get delivered to the big boats?" Mary asked.

Her mom continued. "Today, the marine post office uses a special mailboat. The name of the mailboat is the *J.W. Westcott* II, but everyone calls it the *Westcott*. Because boats can pass by the marine post office any time of the day or night, the *Westcott* never rests. The *Westcott* and her crew work every single day— including nights, weekends, and holidays—throughout the entire shipping season."

"Are there any other mailboats?" Mary wondered.

"Well," her mother answered, "there are other marine post offices and other mailboats in the United States, but the *Westcott* is the only one that delivers the mail directly to the big boats while they are moving. The marine post office even has its own ZIP code."

"Before each boat passes by the marine post office, the *Westcott* is carefully loaded with mail and packages."

"Then the mighty little *Westcott* heads out to meet each boat as it moves up or down the river."

"The crew on the *Westcott* has to be very careful that the mailboat is not damaged when it comes alongside the big boats."

"Once the *Westcott* is next to a big boat, the two must keep moving alongside each other while the mail delivery is made. Sailors lower a rope with a large pail attached to it. The pail is full of mail ready to go ashore. The crew of the *Westcott* takes the mail going ashore out of the pail, and fills it with mail for the crew of the big boat. The sailors then pull the pail back up aboard the big boat. That is why they call it 'mail by the pail.'"

"After the mail has been delivered, the crews of both boats wave goodbye. The Captain on the big boat blows the whistle to say 'Thank you,' and the Captain on the *Westcott* blows the whistle to say 'You're welcome.'"

"Oh! Now I get how it works!" Mary said. Now that Mary understood what mail by the pail meant, she could not wait to send a birthday card to her dad. She began with a blank piece of white paper, then carefully colored, cut, glued, and taped everything together. She took extra time so it would be the perfect card for her father.

When Mary had finished her birthday card, her mom helped her address the envelope.

First, Mary put her name and address in the upper left corner.

Next, she put the special address for her father's boat in the center.

Then Mary placed a postage stamp in the upper right corner.

When the envelope was ready, Mary put a happy face sticker on it. She placed the card in the envelope, sealed it tight, and Mary and her mother took it to the mailbox.

Just as her mother had said, two days later the card was delivered to the marine post office.

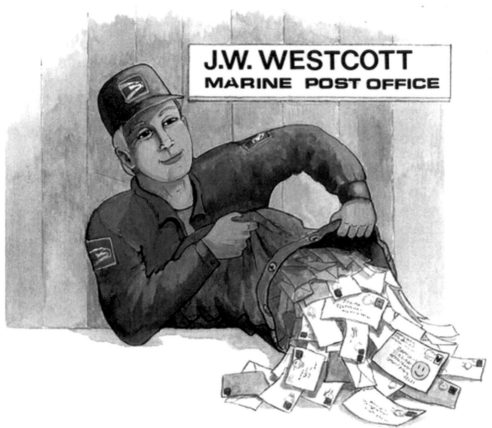

Mary's card waited there another four days before it was put on the *Westcott* and taken out to her dad's big boat as it passed by Detroit.

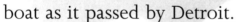

At last the card was placed into the pail along with the rest of the mail and hauled up onto the *Big Laker*.

After the mail delivery was made, the Captain of the *Big Laker* blew the whistle to say "Thank you," and the Captain of the *Westcott* blew the whistle to say "You're welcome."

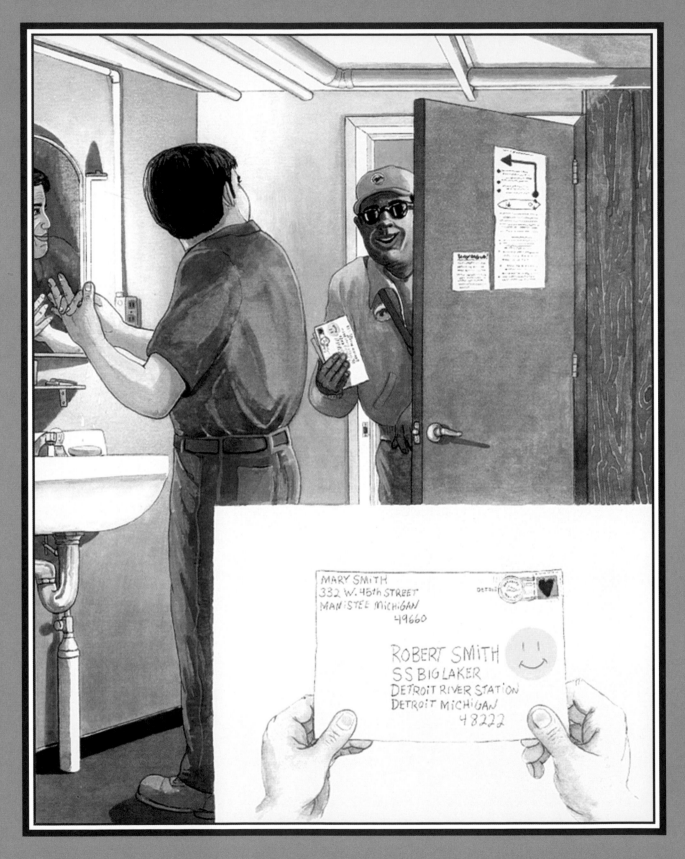

On the *Big Laker*, the mail and packages were sorted. Mary's dad was washing his hands before dinner when Mary's card was delivered to him.

Mary's dad got a big smile on his face when he opened the envelope and saw his special birthday card. This was the best thing he had ever received from the mailboat! That night, he brought Mary's card with him to dinner.

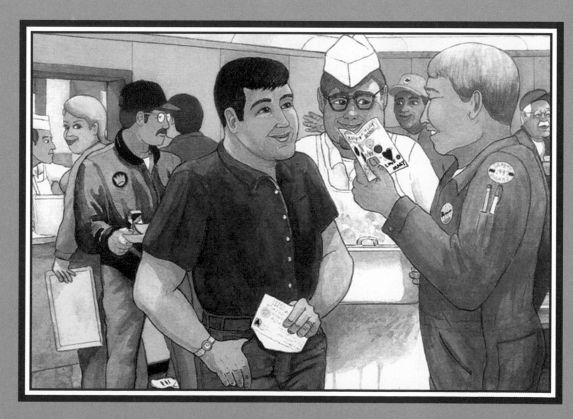

After dinner, Mary's dad put the card on top of his dresser so he could look at it whenever he wanted.

The *Westcott* made a lot of other deliveries that day. For many sailors on the Great Lakes, it was just another chance to get a letter or package from home. But that day, for Mary and her dad, it was a very special delivery of the mail by the pail.

John Ward Westcott started the J. W. Westcott Company in Detroit, Michigan, in 1874. The company boats carried important messages directing a vessel to its next port or cargo.

For most of the nineteenth century, sailors on the Great Lakes received mail only when their boat was at a dock. The U.S. Postal Service improved mail delivery for Great Lakes sailors when they began the marine post office in Detroit in 1895. Over the next fifty-three years, the postal service had many different firms provide mail delivery to the vessels on the Detroit River. Finally, on July 1, 1948, the J. W. Westcott Company was selected to deliver the mail, and they have done so ever since.

The 46-foot-long *J. W. Westcott II* was built in Erie, Pennsylvania, and was specifically designed as a mailboat. The *Westcott*'s large cabin allows it to carry the mail for more than one boat at a time. It was also built with extra large doors that make it easy to handle large items. Today, in addition to delivering the mail, the *Westcott* also delivers packages, newspapers, nautical supplies, groceries, crew members, and even an occasional pizza.

The *Westcott* operates from its dock near the Ambassador Bridge on the Detroit River. During the winter months, when the Great Lakes freeze over, shipping on the Lakes and mail delivery on the Detroit River both come to a halt. Mail service usually begins around the first week in April and runs twenty-four hours a day, seven days a week, until the middle of December.

Tragedy struck the *Westcott* on October 23, 2001, while servicing a saltwater tanker. Two crew members, Captain Catherine Nasiatka and Deckhand David Lewis, lost their lives when the *Westcott* sank in 30 feet of water in the Detroit River. The *Westcott* was raised from the bottom of the river two days later. During the winter, the *Westcott* was completely refurtbised and returned to service on April 8, 2002.

Since the accident, seeing the *Westcott* resume mail deliveries brings feelings of both sadness and joy. Catherine and David will forever be associated wtih the *Westcott*, and everyone in the Great Lakes maritime community will miss them. Yet the repainted and rebulit *J. W. Westcott II* once again serves as a lifeline between the families on shore and the sailors on the freighters. Even in the age of cell phones, satellite phones, and e-mail, every sailor eagerly anticipates passing by Detroit in hopes of receiving a letter or package from home. Hardly a day goes by that someone in the crew doesn't ask, "Hey, Mate! What time will we be at the mailboat?" Although the *Westcott* is small in size compared to the large lake freighters, most sailors agree the mailboat stands tall in the hearts of those who work on the Great Lakes.

A special thank you goes to all those responsible for making the *J. W. Westcott II* one of the most reliable, dependable, and unique mail carriers in the world.

—C.B.

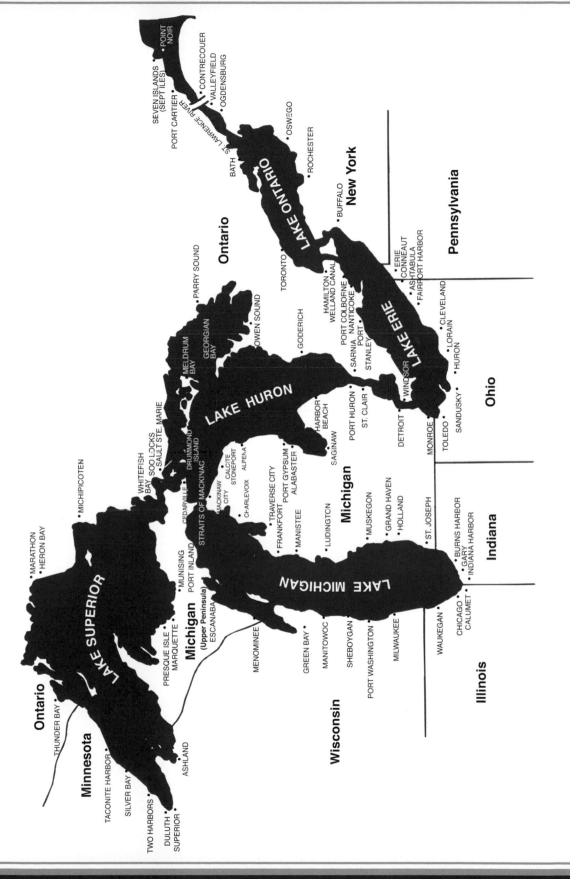

Colin Bergel is a merchant marine deck officer on the Great Lakes and works for the Oglebay Norton Company. When he is not sailing he lives with his family in Manistee, Michigan. This is his first children's book.

Mark Koenig illustrated *Our Michigan Adventure* (Hillsdale Publishing, 1999) and has also illustrated a poster for the city of Manistee. He works in the paper industry and lives with his family in Manistee, Michigan.